The Is Skye

JARROLD

The First Visitors to Skye. The earliest archaeological evidence of habitation on the Isle of Skye dates from about 3000 BC. Neolithic farmers reached Skye from as far away as the Mediterranean, having travelled there by sea along the Atlantic shores of Ireland and western Scotland. A thousand years later, another race – bigger and more round-headed than the first – arrived from the Rhine and Low Countries, bringing with them a semi-nomadic way of life. Celtic settlements began to establish themselves during the first millennium BC and signs of their culture, including brochs (distinctively Scottish defence structures) and impressive castles, can still be seen today.

The Vikings. Around the eighth century, the Vikings, driven from their own homes by overpopulation, invaded Skye, and a period of unrest lasting several centuries began. Today, a number of Skye inhabitants have distinctive fair hair and blue eyes, a sign of the intermarrying between the native dwellers and the Norse settlers. Under the rule of Somerled, the first Celtic Lord of the Isles, and his descendants, Skye maintained its independence from the Scottish kings until the Battle of the Largs which took place in 1263. This finally put an end to the Norse power on the island, but not to the unrest.

In the hands of the Lords of the Isles, scuffles and battles persisted on the island until the end of the fifteenth century, when their power was broken by James IV. In 1540, James V descended on Skye and 'did so terrify those islanders that it brought along peace and quietness to those places afterwards' – but the peace was short-lived, and clan battles did not die down until well into the seventeenth century.

1745 onwards. After the Jacobite rising, life on the island fluctuated greatly. Although the island had never been particularly prosperous, the hardy islanders did not want for lack of life's essentials, and it was not until the eighteenth century that there was any sign of actual destitution. An increasing population and a slowness to adopt new primary industries were probably the main causes. However, over the years and following several official reports and Acts of Parliament, new industries were undertaken, including crofting and sheep farming, kelp harvesting, and the development of fishing for commercial purposes.

Skye Today. Today, as always, Skye possesses an unusual beauty and magnetism which appeal to the loyalty of the native and the romantic inclination of the tourist. Although the rugged economies of the island forces many of its young people to seek their fortunes elsewhere, those born and bred on the island nevertheless retain a deep affection for it, and more and more people now visit it in the summer. The impact of its scenery is spectacular. The Black Cuillins, often shrouded in mist, rise remote and mysterious, the highest peak, Sgurr Alasdair, reaching 995 m (3,300 ft). The three main townships are Portree (the capital), Broadford and Kyleakin, and even these are remarkably small. Most of the inhabitants live in little crofting villages, quite unlike any to be seen outside crofting areas, and the rest are divided between the three larger towns.

Trade. For centuries, Skye was almost self-supporting, and it was not until pedlars started to bring their wares over from the mainland that the islanders were even aware of the existence of some commodities. The first shop was opened at the beginning of the nineteenth century at Kyleakin, and from then the retail business grew rapidly. Meal, oil, tea and tobacco were brought by steamers, and were exchanged for local produce. The availability of goods produced the demand for them, and bit by bit Skye entered into the business of trading. Today, many townships depend on the mobile shops – vans carrying all kinds of goods which call two or three times a week.

Car Ferry Services. Skye is well provided with good ferry services linking it to the mainland and surrounding islands, and bus and coach services connecting the ports with other townships. The busiest ferry service crosses the strait between Lochalsh and Kyleakin, the shortest route from the mainland. (*See picture below.*) This service, now greatly improved to cope with heavy summer traffic, was in existence as early as 1841, though according to one traveller at the time, it was 'detestable, at least for carriages'! The ruins of Castle Moil (*previous page*) are visible from the ferry; dating back to the tenth century it was once known as Dunakin and served as a lookout post and fortress against invading Norsemen. Another ferry runs from Mallaig to Armadale on the Sleat peninsula, seat of the MacDonald Clan, and in the summer only a service operates between Kylerhea and Glenelg, which can be reached via a small turning off the A87 at Shiel Bridge. A ferry goes from just east of Sconser to the Island of Raasay, and from Uig Bay (in the north of the island) a round trip to Lochmaddy on North Uist and Tarbert on Harris is available. Today's visitor can also fly to Skye to the airstrip situated between Broadford and Kyleakin. For up-to-the-minute information on all the services available, contact the Tourist Office in Portree.

Above: *Boarding the Kyleakin-Lochalsh ferry on Skye*
Ci-dessus: *Le car-ferry Kyleakin-Lochalsh sur l'île de Skye*
Oben: *Die Kyleakin-Lochalsh Fähre auf Skye*

Above: *Otters can be seen in their natural environment at the Kylerhea Otter Haven (Photo: F. W. Hogan)*
Ci-dessus: *Au refuge de loutres à Kylerhea, on voit le loutre dans son milieu naturel (Photo: F. W. Hogan)*
Oben: *Im Kylerhea Seeotter-Biotop können Seeotter in ihrer natürlichen Umgebung gesehen werden (Foto: F. W. Hogan)*

Below: *Near Isleornsay, looking across the Sound of Sleat*
Ci-dessus: *Vue, près d'Isleornsay, sur le détroit de Sleat*
Unten: *In der Nähe von Isleornsay, mit Blick über den Sound of Sleat*

Above: *The stables at the Clan Donald Centre*
Ci-dessus: *Les écuries au Centre Clan Donald*
Oben: *Die Ställe im Clan Donald Centre*

The Sleat Peninsula. The green and fertile coastline of this peninsula can rightfully be called the 'Garden of Skye'. Armadale Castle is the second largest castle on Skye, owned by the MacDonalds of Sleat from early times and now the site of the worldwide Clan Donald Centre, set in lovely woodland gardens. The magnificent newly restored stables house a fine restaurant, shop and luxurious letting flats. The visitor can see a Museum of the Isles and an excellent audio-visual. The car-ferry service at Armadale Pier forms another link with the mainland. The road from Armadale follows the coast through Isleornsay from where the tiny island of the same name, with its lighthouse and remains of a small nunnery, can be seen. On its way to Kinloch and Broadford it passes the hamlet of Teangue. Here, on a rocky headland above Knock Bay, stand the ruins of Knock Castle and a short distance further on, a rough and hilly road turns off

inland and heads towards Ord and Tokavaig (*right*). This area is one of great natural beauty. Tokavaig wood, once a Druid oak grove, is protected by the Nature Conservancy as a site of special scientific interest. There are well-established oaks and ash trees here, along with bird cherry and hawthorn, and orchids blossom in the spring.

Above and below left: *The ferry* Pioneer *leaving Armadale for Mallaig*
Ci-dessus et en bas à gauche: *Le ferry* Pioneer *quittant Armadale pour Mallaig*
Oben und unten links: *Die Fähre* Pioneer *beim Auslaufen von Armadale nach Mallaig*

Below: *Tokavaig, an area of great natural beauty*
Ci-dessous: *Tokavaig, région d'une grande beauté naturelle*
Unten: *Tokavaig, eine Gegend von außerordentlicher landschaftlicher Schönheit*

Ancient Rocks and Croft Houses. Midway between Luib and Elgol as the crow flies are the majestic peaks of Blaven, or *Blà Bheinn* in Gaelic, a preview to the impressive Black Cuillins which lie further to the west. From Torrin on the road from Elgol to Broadford, one can gaze across Loch Slapin (*below*) at what is probably the most spectacular view of these black rock faces (*bottom left*). They provide challenging ascents for climbers, particularly the notorious Clach Glas ridge. The main road follows the shores of the loch southwards towards Elgol on the shores of Loch Scavaig (*overleaf*). It is from here that Bonnie Prince Charlie left Skye for good, and half a mile to the south is the cave in which he hid before his departure.

Above left: *Broadford, a good touring centre for the south of the island*
Ci-dessus à gauche: *Broadford, excellente base pour la visite du sud de l'île*
Oben links: *Broadford, Haupt-Ausflugszentrum im Süden der Insel*

Left: *The rugged face of Blà Bheinn*
A gauche: *La façade découpée de Blà Bheinn*
Links: *Die verwitterte Oberfläche des Massivs Blà Bheinn*

Above: *The shores of Loch Slapin*
Ci-dessus: *Les berges du Loch Slapin*
Oben: *Die Ufer des Loch Slapin*

Elgol on the shores of Loch Scavaig
Elgol, sur les bords de Loch Scavaig
Elgol am Ufer des Loch Scavaig

Above: *A traditional 'black house' at Luib*
Ci-dessus: *Une «maison noire» traditionelle à Luib*
Oben: *Eine traditionelle „schwarze Hütte" bei Luib*

Below: *A dramatic view of the Cuillins from Glen Brittle (Photo: J. Ackroyd)*
Ci-dessous: *De Glen Brittle la vue des Cuillins est spectaculaire (Photo: J. Ackroyd)*
Unten: *Eine spektakuläre Ansicht der Cuillins von Glen Brittle aus gesehen (Foto: J. Ackroyd)*

At Luib there is an ancient croft dwelling house once known as a 'black house', now a small museum depicting the early life of a crofter on Skye. These black houses were made by building two stone walls with a gap between and filling the cavity with earth. The thatch was held in place by ropes attached to heavy stones and was used as fertiliser when a replacement was required. Inside, there was a kitchen and living room at one end, an area often housing the family's animals at the other, and a room with a box-bed in-between.

Loch Ainhort to Glen Brittle. One of the most spectacular areas of Skye, the Cuillin range *(bottom left)* lies between Glen Brittle to the west, and the main road leading from Broadford to Sligachan in the east. This road passes through Luib and follows the shores of Loch Ainhort before cutting inland beneath Lord MacDonald's Forest and Glamaig as it heads towards Portree. Loch Ainhort is also served by a small byroad which runs the whole perimeter of the loch and along the coast, joining the main road just east of Sconser. Glen Brittle and the little road that runs north towards Loch Harport marks the western reaches of the Cuillins. From here, magnificent views of the black hills rising steeply from the green valley of the River Brittle are to be had. The Forestry Commission has acquired land in Glen Brittle, and the plantations are witness to their work. Although it is thought that a thousand years ago Skye was densely forested, without regular and scientific planting today, the island would soon become bare of trees. These plantations provide regular employment on the island, and the more mature trees are felled for use as wood-pulp. Not easily accessible, Glen Brittle remains something of a nature sanctuary. The goldcrest may be heard here in the spring, and the raven *(fitheach in Gaelic)* is common in the plantations.

Above: Loch Ainhort is situated in one of the most spectacular areas of Skye
Ci-dessus: Le Loch Ainhort est situé dans l'une des régions les plus spectaculaires de l'île
Oben: Loch Ainhort liegt in einem der landschaftlich schönsten Gebiete von Skye

The Red and Black Cuillins. The River Sligachan flows through the U-shaped glacial valley of Glen Sligachan and forms a boundary of the Black and Red Cuillins. Also known as the Coolins or Cuchullins, possibly after an Ossianic hero, the main ridges of this range – the Black Cuillins – extend over this south-west corner of the island. They overlook many views of panoramic splendour, including Loch Coruisk which was described by Scott in the *Lord of the Isles*. They form a six-mile semicircle of black gabbro, coarse crystalline rocks that have formed into vertical joints. Some fifteen peaks reach a height of over 900 m (3,000 ft); these are known as 'Munros' after H. T. Munro who first listed them in 1890. The highest peak is that of Sgurr Alasdair at 995 m (3,300 ft), but perhaps the most interesting is Sgurr Gillean with its strange jagged and pinnacled outline. The Red Cuillins, facing the main ridge, contrast greatly with the black semicircle. Called 'red', they are in fact composed of pink granite which

weathers to smooth rounded forms, quite different from the jagged outlines of
the gabbro. The view of Glamaig from the road heading north after Loch Ainhort
is well worthwhile: its simple outline is capped by a summit of basalt lava, and
reaches a height of 770 m (2,530 ft); Lord MacDonald's Forest and the peak of
Marsco form the background. Ptarmigan and snow bunting can be seen in the
unspoilt mountain ranges, and a number of rare alpine plants grow there,
including the alpine rock cress, found nowhere else in Britain. The Cuillins are
of great interest to geologists, climbers and tourists alike, and their outline can
be seen from the loftier peaks on the mainland.

Above: *The Red Cuillins are actually composed of weathered pink granite*
Ci-dessus: *Les Cuillins rouges sont en fait constituées de granit rose altéré*
Oben: *Die Red Cuillins verdanken ihren Namen dem verwitterten rosa Granit*

N

Duntulm Castle
Kilmaluag
Flora Macdonald Monument
Kilmuir
Museum of Island Life
Quiraing
Flodigarry
Staffin

A855

SOUND OF RAASAY

...OUND

TROTTERNISH

THE STORR

Bernisdale
Skeabost Bridge

Kingsburgh

PORTREE

A855

Uig Bay
Uig

Ferries to the
Western Isles

Loch Losait
Loch
Greshornish

Loch
Snizort

A850

B885

VATERNISH

Halistra

Dunvegan Castle
Dunvegan

Bracadale

Loch...

Loch Dunvegan

Loch
Bracadale

Milovaig

B884

Macleod's
Tables

Climbing in the Cuillins. Scaling the hills of Skye is not a venture to be undertaken lightly. The gabbro rock, with its rough surface and jutting ledges, is relatively safe for climbers, but the steep ascents, the vagaries of the weather, and, in the Red Cuillins, the screes, demand some skill and experience of mountaineering. One of the first climbers in the Cuillins, the Rev. C. Lesingham Smith, had to crawl on his hands and knees and remarked that 'a single false step would have hurled us to destruction'. During these early years, a certain pioneering spirit prevailed, and as each new peak was conquered, new feats of mountaineering endurance were sought. While in 1911 the completion of the 'Great Traverse' in twelve hours was considered quite a feat, by 1960 climbers were attempting the return journey, including an extra 1,200 m (4,000 ft) of ascent and a descent to sea-level, in under twenty-four hours!

With the increasing popularity of climbing in the Cuillins, mountain rescue has become an important service. On Skye, it is organised by the police, but despite their efficiency, each year brings new climbing accidents. It is therefore essential that all climbers should protect themselves as well as possible. Clothing that seems adequate at sea-level is likely to prove quite insufficient up in the mountains, and weatherproof garments and the correct footwear must be worn. It is always a good idea to travel in threes so that in the case of an accident, one person can stay with the casualty while the third goes for help. Adequate supplies of food, a torch, a whistle and a contour map are important things to carry with you.

Above: *View across bay to Raasay*
Ci-dessus: *Vue sur la baie à Raasay*
Oben: *Blick über bai zu Raasay*

From Sligachan. The area around Sligachan provides an excellent spot from which to view a variety of Skye scenery. The page before the map shows several of the Cuillin peaks, and the village of Sligachan itself affords a superb view. In Victorian days, it was the main gathering point for the enthusiastic climbers setting out to conquer the Cuillins, and Sligachan Inn dates from this time.

From the mouth of Loch Sligachan one can look out on the island of Raasay, the largest of the fifty or so islands and islets which surround Skye. Many of the plants originally thought only to be found on Skye grow on Raasay, including the mountain avens, the common wintergreen and the cowberry or red whortleberry. Iron ore was once mined there, but the main occupation is agriculture, although in the winter months hay often has to be imported from Skye to feed the livestock.

Heading west from Sligachan, the A863 heads towards Loch Harport (*below*) and on to Bracadale and Dunvegan further north. The Talisker Distillery stands on the shores of the loch and forms an attractive set of buildings. It is one of the few manually operated distilleries left, and the stills, made of gleaming copper, are an impressive sight.

Below: *Strange lights at sunset over Loch Harport*
Ci-dessous: *Coucher de soleil spectaculaire sur Loch Harport*
Unten: *Lichtzaubereien beim Sonnenuntergang über Loch Harport*

Above: *The Square, Portree*
Ci-dessus: The Square *(la Place), à Portree*
Oben: *Der Marktplatz von Portree*

Below: *Cottages along the waterfront at Portree*
Ci-dessous: *Cottages au bord de l'eau à Portree*
Unten: *Cottages am Rande des Wassers in Portree*

The Town of Portree. Portree is the largest town on Skye and the principal shopping centre for both the islanders and visitors. Its name denotes 'King's Harbour' and recalls a visit by James V, father of Mary Queen of Scots. Many fishing boats can be seen in the harbour, Portree is a busy port as well as an important centre for many diverse activities. The dramatic ten-mile-long mountain ridge known as The Storr (*overleaf*) lies to the north, with the Old Man of Storr, a 45 m (150 ft) high pillar of rock, below. Until the nineteenth century the town was virtually non-existent and it was Sir James MacDonald and successive MacDonald chiefs who laid the foundations for the town as it is today. The present Royal Hotel stands on the site of Mac Nab's Inn where Prince Charlie said his farewells to Flora MacDonald before leaving for Raasay. Meall House which looks out over the harbour is the oldest listed building; now the Tourist Information Office, it was once used as a prison, although crime was never a problem on Skye. In 1840 for example, the jail held sixteen prisoners, only five of whom had committed crimes for personal gain. One of Skye's visitor centres is the Skye Wool Mill – originally the Hogg Woollen Mill, started in 1880 – located just outside Portree.

Large colonies of rooks and jackdaws are to be found near Portree.

Above: *Portree harbour*
Ci-dessus: *Le port de Portree*
Oben: *Der Hafen von Portree*

The ten-mile-long ridge of The Storr, one of Skye's most dramatic natural features
La crête du mont Storr, longue de seize kilomètres, l'une des curiosités de Skye
Die 16 Kilometer lange Bergkette The Storr, dramatisches Naturmerkmal auf der Insel

The Quiraing. The A855 heads north from Portree along the eastern coast of the Trotternish peninsula, joining up with the A856 to form a full circular route. Apart from the Cuillins, most of Skye is composed of basalt lava, and the most imposing formations of this are to be found here. At the northern end of the peninsula, the Quiraing can only be reached on foot, but the splendid views over the Trotternish hills and the Torridon mountains of the mainland make the walk well worthwhile. Its many pillars and ridges make it look like a group of hills in miniature. An unusual grass-covered rock known as The Table is surrounded by a natural amphitheatre, and in front of this the sharp pinnacle called The Needle Rock rises to 37 m (120 ft). In the depths of this strange and wild countryside alpine gardens blossom, including plants such as moss campion, roseroot, purple and mossy saxifrage, the three-flowered rush and the attractive globe flower. For centuries, many of Skye's native plants have been used as foods, medicines and dyes. The Skye Museum of Island Life at Kilmuir (*below*), situated in the north-west of Trotternish, displays a list of some of these. It constitutes five beautifully restored, traditionally styled thatched croft houses, containing examples of early domestic appliances and agricultural implements, such as the *caschrom,* the traditional Hebridean foot plough.

Above left: *The Skye Heritage Centre lies in beautiful Portree Forest*
Ci-dessus, à gauche: *Le Skye Heritage Centre dans la magnifique forêt de Portree*
Oben links: *Das Skye Heritage Centre liegt im herrlichen Portree Forest*

Left: *Near Staffin, in the Trotternish Peninsula*
A gauche: *Près de Staffin, péninsule de Trotternish*
Links: *In der Nähe von Staffin, auf der Halbinsel Trotternish*

Above: *Skye Museum of Island Life, Kilmuir*
Ci-dessus: *Musée de la Vie dans l'Ile de Skye, à Kilmuir*
Oben: *Heimatmuseum der Insel Skye, Kilmuir*

Above: *The dramatic Mealt Falls, with Kilt Rock in the background*
Ci-dessus: *Les chutes spectaculaires du Mealt et, à l'arrière-plan, le rocher Kilt Rock*
Oben: *Die eindrucksvollen Mealt Falls vor der Kulisse des Kilt Rock*

The Trotternish Peninsula. Before reaching the Quiraing, the A855 passes close to the impressive ten-mile ridge of The Storr. Wild crags and lofty peaks offer magnificent views over the Cuillins to the south and the Outer Hebrides to the west. The Old Man of Storr, a detached pinnacle beneath The Storr, rises to 45 m (150 ft). The whole peninsula is rich in association with Bonnie Prince Charlie, and a memorial to Flora MacDonald (*bottom left*), the prince's famous companion, lies in the churchyard just beyond the Skye Museum of Island Life. At great risk to her own personal safety, she came to his rescue after his defeat at the Battle of Culloden in April 1746.

Close by, on the coast road between Kilmuir and Portree, is a steep and dangerous cliff known as Kilt Rock, near which cascades a magnificent waterfall (*top left*).

Travelling south from Kilmuir, the road climbs Idrigill Hill and makes a steep descent through a double hairpin bend towards Uig and Uig Bay (*top right*). Before this, a minor road crosses the Quiraing to Staffin Bay, penetrating deep into the heart of its strangely formed hills and precipices.

Shellfish are an important catch on Skye, and often Norwegian ships come to the port of Uig to collect prawn tails. The trade has proved very profitable for Uig, although it is only seasonal.

Just beyond Uig on the A856 back to Portree, a little *cul-de-sac* on the left leads to a place called Fairy Glen (*bottom right*), a collection of caves in a small river valley, with a loch nearby. The weird and grotesque shapes of the rocks and the strange atmosphere that prevails do indeed make it seem feasible that the glen is inhabited by the 'little people'.

Left: *Flora MacDonald, brave companion of Bonnie Prince Charlie*
A gauche: *Flora MacDonald, compagne courageuse de Bonnie Prince Charlie*
Links: *Flora MacDonald, die treue Begleiterin von Bonnie Prince Charlie*

Above: *Uig Bay. A ferry service operates from here to the Outer Hebrides*
Ci-dessus: *La baie d'Uig d'où part un ferry-boat pour les îles occidentales*
Oben: *Uig Bay: eine Fähre verkehrt von hier zu den Äußeren Hebriden*

Below: *Fairy Glen, so named for its 'Faerie-land' appearance and atmosphere*
Ci-dessous: *Fairy Glen, ainsi nommée pour son atmosphère «féerique»*
Unten: *Das nach seiner märchenhaften Atmosphäre genannte Glen Fairy*

Above: *Golden sunset over Loch Snizort, Skye's largest sea loch*
Ci-dessus: *Coucher de soleil sur le Loch Snizort, le plus grand lac de mer de Skye*
Oben: *Sonnenuntergang am Loch Snizort, Skyes größtem Salzwassersee*

Below: *Loch Greshornish, on the road to Dunvegan, seen from Flashader*
Ci-dessous: *Loch Greshornish, sur la route de Dunvegan, vu de Flashader*
Unten: *Blick von Flashader auf Loch Greshornish an der Straße nach Dunvegan*

The Vaternish Promontory. As one heads north into this wild promontory, one is aware of a landscape strikingly different from Trotternish, although both are composed of basalt lava. Here, undulating moorland is dotted with pinnacles and queer flat-topped hills, and an occasional crofters' township, isolated but friendly. Loch Snizort (*top left*) is a typical drowned valley and quite different in character from the generally narrow sea lochs. The island's deepest indentation, it separates Vaternish from Trotternish to the east. The eider nests here, having extended its territory across the Minch from the west coast of Uist, and the barnacle goose sometimes pays winter visits to the Ascrib Isles in the outer loch. Greylag geese were believed to have nested here until 1867. Loch Losait (*below*), an inlet at the north end of Loch Snizort, can be reached along a byroad from Halistra. There are no main roads on the promontory, but the A850 runs past the head of Loch Greshornish (*bottom left*) through Flashader to Dunvegan on the west. The western coastline is accessible by road, though only a minor one, as far as Trumpan. In 1597, the MacDonalds of Uist set fire to the church here, killing all but one of the MacLeod congregation; they in turn suffered heavily when the ebb-tide prevented their escape. The ruins of the church are still to be seen, lonely in their isolated setting.

Above: *Loch Losait, accessible by a small road from Halistra*
Ci-dessus: *Loch Losait, où l'on se rend par une petite route au départ de Halistra*
Oben: *Loch Losait ist auf einer schmalen Straße von Halistra aus zu erreichen*

Dunvegan to Bracadale. From Halistra, the view stretches across Dunvegan Loch to Dunvegan Head, and further south is the hamlet of Stein on the shores of Loch Bay (*below*). One of the first fishing stations was established here in 1787 following a report by John Knox who toured the island in the 1780s. The project was a failure however, the islanders being quite content to catch only what they needed. At the point where three roads and three rivers meet between Vaternish and Dunvegan is the famous Fairy Bridge where, legend has it, the fairy wife of a MacLeod chief – pining for the land of Faerie – left him to return there. Dunvegan Castle (*opposite*) is the seat of the Clan MacLeod and thanks to the efforts of Dame Flora MacLeod, has become a worldwide centre of reunion for members of the clan. The original structure still stands but the inside has been completely modernised. Many fascinating relics are on display here, including the Fairy Flag, said to possess miraculous powers for members of the clan, family portraits and items associated with the Bonnie Prince.

From Dunvegan, the A863 skirts the shores of sheltered Loch Bracadale. One of the finest harbours on the island, it is also used as a breeding ground by the common and the grey, or Atlantic, seal (*right, below*).

Above: *Loch Bay, from the little fishing centre of Stein*
Ci-dessus: *Loch Bay, vu du petit port de pêche de Stein*
Oben: *Loch Bay von dem kleinen Fischerort Stein aus gesehen*

Above right: *Dunvegan Castle, now completely modernised inside*
A droite en haut: *Le château de Dunvegan, à l'intérieur entièrement restauré*
Oben rechts: *Dunvegan Castle ist im Inneren völlig modernisiert*

Below right: *Grey seal pup. Skye's shores team with marine life (Photo: L. Campbell)*
A droite en bas: *Jeune phoque gris. Le littoral de Skye possède une abondante vie marine (Photo: L. Campbell)*
Unten rechts: *Graues Seerobbenbaby. An Skyes Küsten wimmelt es von den verschiedensten Meerestieren (Foto: L. Campbell)*

Above: *Footpath to Camasunary (Photo: M. Nicholl)*
Ci-dessus: *Sentier menant à Camasunary (Photo: M. Nicholl)*
Oben: *Fußweg nach Camasunary (Foto: M. Nicholl)*

Below: *Sunset over Skye*
Ci-dessous: *Coucher de soleil sur Skye*
Unten: *Sonnenuntergang über Skye*